Change
Your
Behavior

Change
Your
Life

Published by Mindstir Media, LLC
45 Lafayette Rd | Suite 181| North Hampton, NH 03862 | USA
1.800.767.0531 | www.mindstirmedia.com

Printed in the United States of America
ISBN-13: 978-1-7339571-8-2
Library of Congress Control Number on file with the publisher

Change Your Behavior Change Your Life

Rhonda White

Table of *Contents*

Dr. Martin Luther King Jr.

*A man whose behavior never changed
in spite of his many challenges. He enriched my life.*

Rhonda White

FOREWORD
from Dana Dorfman

When Rhonda White first came to me to discuss the concept of behavior, I was drawn to her thinking. Soft spoken with earnest dedication topping her voice, I detected her heart was consumed with little else but to talk to people about their behavior. So, this is the true emphasis of her book. Rhonda clearly gives a message that no one should have a compromised heart when they deal with the subject of behavior.

If people behaved better they would always have a better chance at life's successes and this immediately became the message of her book. It takes a lot to change society but it doesn't take a lot to change your behavior. Rhonda White's sincere professional tones are moving and admiring. It has been my pleasure to be a consultant to her with this book. "Change Your Behavior Change Your Life". Life definitely puts its arm around her in a special way.

Sincerely,

Dana Dorfman
Behavior Consultant

Dedications

This is dedicated to those of you who recognize that bad behavior is an epidemic that has plagued our society with violence. Bad behavior has also attacked our personal finance, health, family, friends, and careers.

I ask you dear reader, has it attacked you personally? If so this book is for you. I bring you:

"Change your behavior, Change your life."

Dear reader you must prepare for the speed bumps in life. Good behavior is a great stabilizing force. Learn, love and focus! At times, life can seem like it is falling apart, but in actuality it could be positioning you for a better place. You must breathe, stay calm and work on creating the best version of you. It can be done; I did it and so can you. I say to you dear reader "Change your behavior Change your life!

Rhonda White

Acknowledgments

Love the gift of life that God has given you. "God is faithful; he will not let you be tempted beyond what you can bear. But when you are tempted, he will also provide a way out so that you can stand up under it." Corinthians 10:13". Thank you to my family and friends who remind me of this verse.

Thank-you to the wind beneath my wings
Jeff, Krystal, Viola (mom)
and Skye our loving Family puppy

Special thank you to my circle of influencers

Rhonda White

PREFACE

Dear Reader,

Behavior is a journey. You've got that right!

My behavior has been a very long journey and it is still under way today. Every single day I work on my behavior. It is hard work let me tell you. It is important work. I know I want to be the best that I can be, and I am aware that my behavior must always be at its best. My behavior is a reflection of me. If negative behavior is the controlling factor in my life then I won't meet my life's expectations. This will cause me to make rash decisions. I would never want my behavior to take my smile away. Yes! It could steal my joy.

Should my bad behavior take over, I will not make progress. I also know there is a good chance that I won't be holding the elevator open for anyone and I won't be cordial. I may be irrational in my judgements and my conduct may very well be unfeeling. If bad behavior is controlling me, I know that I will not be as concerned for the welfare of others as I should be. Those responses will not be appropriate to the changes and challenges of my life.

Therefore, I cannot and will not allow bad behavior to

take hold of me. Every single day I must make a commitment to the betterment of good behavior. I will do everything I can on this planet to make sure that my behavior is a mirror of who I am. I will take pride in my rational way of thinking, both personally and professionally and most of all; I will treat people with respect. To do this, I must make sure that my behavior is coming from a good place.

I must admit there was a point in my life where my behavior was being challenged. I felt tested and I knew it was time to breathe and focus. I did not want to react without thinking. My world was complex. I had no choice but to keep my behavior in check and take a more refined approach to my situations or be buried by bad behavior.

My earlier marriage was one that certainly presented life changes and disappointments. I did not want it to ruin my professional or my personal life. I am fortunate today that I have moved on. I have a beautiful daughter who is a successful young lady who brings me great joy. Looking back at my childhood, my loving parents raised my siblings and I with love and respect. Our foundation has kept us well connected with one another. My loving mother (Viola Russell) was the pillar to our foundation and still is today!

When you release the negative things in life you release bad behavior. I remember an early recollection in my life that I've never been able to forget and it changed me at a very young age. Chicago born and raised, (I love Chicago and all it has offered me in my life) It has made me realize so many things which has awakened me to what would later become a career interest and subject of this book. I was the new girl in a new school. I was in sixth grade and I remember listening to the teacher in the classroom when someone behind me threw a small rock at the back of my head. Fortunately, I was okay, but a lot hit me in that instance, not just the rock. What hit me was the recognition of bad behavior.

I couldn't believe that someone could do that. I questioned, *"how was that person raised?"* I mean, come on! I remember letting out this loud screech. It was from that point that I can honestly say that bad behavior has always been something that I have glared at in life.

Before I go any further, I must briefly recap milestones in my personal journey. I have lived a life of firsts with poise and presence and have always been proud of my positive moves. A true positive move for me was when I realized my passion for personal development. Education was also a big milestone for me. I was a first-generation graduate earning a Bachelor's degree in Behavioral Science from National Louis University. This was a great accomplishment. It has given me confirmation to what I know to be an inevitable career in the study of people and behavior.

I continued my educational quest earning my Masters in Training and Development from Roosevelt University. Soon after graduating, the flood gates of opportunity afforded me new ways to grow which has always given me a feeling of experiencing the ultimate! It wasn't until I had my daughter that I knew I had truly received the ultimate blessing. Moving forward, I continue to reflect on my educational experience while instilling these values into my amazing daughter who has grown up to be a beautiful and successful young lady and who now holds her MBA and who continues her educational quest for success.

Another milestone for me was when I decided to choose my happiness and file for a divorce. I knew this divorce would pave the way for a better life, believe me it did! My worth and value as a woman was fulfilled. I am happy with me!

Milestones continued from 2013 to 2018 when I was recognized with the following: the Community Leadership award, Women of Excellence award and the Community Catalyst Award. Letters, and calls of appreciation continued to pour in. Each of these milestones was reassurance that I had made the right moves. Lastly, I have been successful in corporate America for thirty plus years … yes!

What kept me going was my faith in God who has guided me through my journey. My perception of who I am was never mistaken or shaken. He has kept me focused on making good decisions. I never want to offend anyone by letting bad behavior or any one with bad behavior change me! Yes I know that's hard. I strived to keep my response my choice….believe me it is your choice! "I know life can make you go there sometimes! But, again make it your choice how you go and how you respond.

Behavior is so personal, yet it has such a massive effect on your life. Wallowing in anger doesn't help you move forward. It is impossible, as a human being, not to drift into occasional bad moods, childish reactions and downright selfishness. Personal growth, stability and loving relationships are all positive gains in your development.

I have learned that it is important to dismantle the situation that is the cause of poor behavior. You cannot get yourself stuck in a dysfunctional cycle of bad behavior. It is so important to acknowledge it, face it and fix it. The severity of your bad behavior inhibits growth and sadly will destroy your character personally and professionally.

So dear reader, don't even go there! If you are struggling and instantly get in a bad mood, if you lost your job and life is coming full circle, and not in a good way, or you are having a rough time of it all, change will come. It breaks through when you least expect it. Never give up on a chance to improve your behavior because I say to you dear reader, don't give up on yourself. Don't lose your way! Inspire yourself to move forward. Grab opportunities that exist. Prosper in the riches of good behavior!

My behavior is the reflection of who I am
If I think more about my behavior
I can think more about you....

Rhonda White

INTRODUCTION

Dear Reader,

Do you feel as if you live in a world where bad behavior has taken over?

Bad behavior is so toxic. If someone just looks out the window and takes a breath of fresh air it could quickly change their behavior. Believe me, I have seen it and witnessed it myself. Guilt and anger are working together when we as human beings should be working together. This epidemic is creating adult temper tantrums for instance: the slamming of doors, banging tables, yelling, screaming along with erratic episodes for no reason.

This behavior is offensive and outlandish. We are highly sensitive to things that people say about us but are we highly sensitive to things you say and do around people. You notice someone else's behavior but you don't notice yours. It is a two-way street, but you are under the aura of bad behavior and you can't make sense of it. Fact is you may be doing things offensively and don't even realize it. Bad behavior will make you think that your behavior is normal. This epidemic of bad behavior is surely on the rise! It is only a matter of time before bad behavior knocks on your door, or has it already knocked? No worry. There is a cure in this book and it has a remedy. Read on!

Changing behaviors is challenging, no doubt about it. Evolving into better version of yourself takes sacrifice, energy, focus and commitment. It takes you to Change your behavior Change your life!

"You are always responsible for how
you act no matter how you feel."
Robert Tew

CHAPTER ONE

Good behavior
Has made me open my eyes
And embrace silence with
A 1 2 3 attitude!
I can yell at you in my mind
But your ears will never hear it
Because I am immune from bad behavior

Rhonda White

. . . .

Someone said I was going the wrong way.
I just looked at them and smiled.
I knew what I was doing.
I wasn't headed the wrong way.
I was going the right way.
I was headed in the direction of good behavior!

Rhonda White

Welcome!

Behavior… We own it… We control it… We can do it!
Change your behavior! Change your life!

Rhonda White

Dear Reader,

This book is the ultimate guide to good behavior. It will teach you how to look at your behavior in a positive light. You will find this book is concise and it will get you where you need to go and that is to a better life with greater opportunities. Now no one can deny that we like hanging around people who we find interesting and attractive. But we also like hanging around people for the wrong reason. I will bet you never thought that you would enjoy being with people because of their behavior. This is a very big part of who you associate with. If you like how someone treats you, you like their behavior. You see dear reader, when a person treats you nicely, are they practicing good behavior are drawn to them.

We all face a world every day that is not filled with the nicest of people. People say terrible things and behave miserably. Bad behavior ruins careers, marriages, friendships and reputations which is very difficult to repair. These people have been affected by bad behavior. Don't let it happen to you because the bad behavior gets into every aspect of your life.

Bad behavior is out there in full force moving rapidly through our society. Every minute, every second every hour. You must go to great lengths to avoid getting trapped in this epidemic of bad behavior. It will make you insensitive with the inability to apologize even though you know that you have been wrong. The bad behavior makes you selfish and the type of person who finds safety and comfort in jealousy and envy. The bad behavior will make your life spiral out of control. I say, dear reader, do not allow this to happen. Nothing good can happen for you, if you don't change your behavior.

The Greek philosopher "Plato" wrote
"Human behavior flows from three main sources:
desires, emotions, and knowledge"

CHAPTER TWO

Someone once told me that champions are not easily offended. Well... I say be a champion of your behavior. You hold the key to who you invite in your life!

Rhonda White

. . . .

Do you often wonder about other people?
And what makes them laugh
What makes them smile or not make them smile?
The only thing we know
About other people
Is what we see and that is their behavior

Rhonda White

Dear Reader,

I say this over and over. I will continue to repeat myself and emphasize my stand on behavior. If I emphasize nothing else in this book, it is that bad behavior is an epidemic, and it is moving rapidly. Bad behavior has people obnoxious, short tempered, loud, emotionally toxic and volatile. Appreciating someone speaking their mind is one thing, but this distinct air of disregard that we breathe in on a regular basis is becoming out of control. It's almost like its airborne and filling the world with disrespect. It is apparent to me people have been struck by these negative dynamics and respect has lost its importance and value. Can you imagine a world without respect?

I am concerned about this epidemic of bad behavior because of my commitment to good behavior. People have deeply-rooted habits and one of these habits is behavior. Have you ever thought about behavior as being a habit. Well, it is. Behavior can be a good habit and it can be a bad habit. If part of your behavior is to visit the sick this is a good habit. Our habits can strengthen us or weaken us. The problem is people don't devote any time to their behavior. So many people don't even think about their behavior. This book calls attention to your behavior in every page.

I am not surprised that people are affected by this epidemic of bad behavior. It is apparent that it is highly contagious, and our road ways are filled with road rage. The expressways are at a dead stop. Everyone is just inching along. Horns are honking; fingers are going up, for pedestrians to hurry up… move on…get out the way. Drivers are tooting their horns at school buses as they impatiently wait for students to get off the school bus or get hit. What the heck is going on? I know it's the bad behavior epidemic.

Is this the kind of behavior you want to leave for the next generation. If you are doing it and they are seeing it they will emulate, magnify and intensify your behavior. Is this what you want? I personally don't want to pass this down to the next generation.

It appears today that manners may be a thing of the past. It seems as if etiquette and respectful behavior doesn't come naturally. Arguably more than ever people appear to be modeling rude behavior that they see around them. If someone is exposed to rude behavior, they seem to pass it on to the next person and so on. You see, this is bad behavior. It just goes around and around and around. Good behavior really must be taught. But this is the issue. Manners are no longer stressed in society. And I do not understand this. Kids get mixed messages and grow up wearing a veil of rudeness and think it is okay.

There is a cure, but you must want to be cured. You must want to throw the rudeness out of your life. Politeness is out there and I'm going to tell you, it's beautiful. It seems like it takes a lot for people to be polite and I wonder why. Do you know why, dear reader? People are too busy doing other things in life and being polite just seems to get in the way. Simply put, people don't have the time to be polite! Politeness has been permanently misplaced. I think the bad behavior has wiped it off the earth!

What has happened to love, respect and downright caring for others. Why is anger so easy and being kind so incredibly difficult. Everyone should feel a responsibility to be kind to others and if you are in this world you should feel a responsibility for your behavior. Bad behavior has its own path. It charts its future differently attacking the weak.

Today's society shines a light brighter than ever on bad behavior. It ripples into every part of our being. It's like bed bugs spreading in the schools, in households, in companies. It even ripples into the treatment of animals, children, and the elderly. How about this, If you are having a bad day, take a step back and pray! If you are having good day share it with someone! You will be surprise how lifting someone else up will lift you up as well.

Read on!

Compliment and praise those who are displaying good behavior. Be compassionate to all people and animals. The inevitable fallout of the bad behavior has huge consequences. Good things happen to those who do good things. Call it karma or whatever you want to call it, If your behavior is deteriorating and at a swelling point, face it and fix it. If you regret your toxic behavior, let people know that you do. Don't keep it a secret own it. I will be addressing the power of journaling. It is a therapeutic release and will help you improve your behavior. But for now, read on.

When people shout and interrupt they are a part of an appalling trend that is taking place in this nation and it is not attractive. This is the epidemic of bad behavior. It is not attractive to throw a tantrum. It is a toxic world for those who are nasty to others, believe me. All I can say is you are better than that. You are better than bad behavior you are displaying. If you don't show consideration for others and you enjoy humiliating people, it is obvious that you have bad behavior; it is time to make a change. This book is here to help you do just that, It's time to change your behavior, change your life.

Getting rid of the bad behavior is vital to your journey here on earth. Bad behavior gives you a reputation. Word gets around about you. A series of rumors end of in the ears and eyes of the "talk-followers" and the "social media trackers". Bad behavior precedes you wherever you go. Reboot your behavior. Become attuned to the new world in your life where your attitude and demeanor are worth talking about. Make bad behavior a thing of the past. You will only come back better and stronger in life when you face your behavior and fix it.

Remember, change your behavior and you will change

your life.

Change your behavior change your attitude
Change your behavior change your image
Change your behavior Change someone else life.
Change your behavior Change your life!

Rhonda White

CHAPTER THREE

Communication is not about making people miserable. It is about making someone understand not only what is explicitly being said but also what is inferred. In other words, be respectful and a good listener. Being perceptive is incredibly important. Effective communication is essential in today's world. So many people cannot communicate effectively, and it is frustrating for all involved in the conversation. Frustration leads to bad behavior.

Communicating with someone is not about manipulating someone. You may not even think you are manipulating the conversation but if you are, right then and there you have lost a business partner, friend, colleague, or a relationship. No one likes to be talked down to, disrespected, interrupted, manipulated and the list goes on and on. Manipulating or attempting to manipulate someone is wrong; this is another example of bad behavior.

It is the art of deception, really. Manipulative people hide behind a mask. They need to control everything and everyone around them this is bad behavior. Now, you may be saying you are not this person; I do not interrupt people. I do not manipulate people and so on. As human beings, we have the tendency to hide our true feelings. You may not realize your tone or your behavior when you are speaking or meeting with people. You may not realize that you are being offensive.

Behavior journaling is really the answer to make you see if you have the traits of someone who handles situations with only you as the priority. And if you don't ask if the problem is you, then I really suggest you journal. You could have traits of bad behavior and you just don't see it. I am introducing this concept to you right here, dear reader.

It is an interesting source for you to outline the basics of who you are. Identify, areas in your behavior that no one can see but you. Let me tell you something, the biggest stranger in your life is you. And when it comes to your behavior, chances are you don't know the power behind jounaling your behavior. This is the reason I have introduced the concept of behavior journaling. Keeping an account of your behavior, you are on your way to changing your behavior!

But, do you know that it is a smart move for you to control your behavior and not allow your behavior to control you. Your behavior interacts with other people. In my thirty plus years in the financial industry, I have had the opportunity to work with people from every walk of life. I've counseled women, couples, youths, millennials, baby boomers, generation X, Y, Z and the list goes on.

I have seen and heard the stories as well as witnessed the breakdown of tears of many. Many times, I find myself consoling, counseling, mentoring, mothering and educating people. I have found one thing that people have in common it lies in the center of your inner being and that is behavior. When it comes to how we handle life challenges or changes. Both areas can be good, challenges you can overcome and changes you can learn to adapt too.

When it comes to your behavior don't get stuck in a bubble otherwise it will deflate and drain your inner most being. Things that are out of your control or you just can't do anything about it, leave it, and move on. Instead focus on things that you can control, namely your behavior.

Getting that dream job, making friends, buying the wardrobe, the new car, it's nice until you get out of control. Sadly your behavior tells you its ok, and what is even worse you avoid it but, I say to you "if you don't face it you will never fix it.

What you may not realize is that your behavior is what makes you look good or bad and it doesn't matter how nice your wardrobe is, believe me. Behavior is the interaction force to inking those deals. Having good behavior may just be the thing that gets you that job. It has been my utmost priority in the writing of this book to provide to you, dear reader, a wonderful and detailed road map to guide you to good behavior.

Unethical behavior has consequences for followers no matter who you are. Leaders, men and women as well as the young and the old. It is about being humble and grounded and appreciative of others and doing the things you love. I do know this for sure we all think we are here for eternity, we are time travelers, we are tourists that is why it is so important for us to begin to make smart moves in our personal life and the lives of the people we love. I emphasize don't wait to get smart tomorrow get smart today. Every day is a day of accomplishment and opportunity. Every day is an opportunity for you to improve your behavior.

When I journal, I feel much better.
I get out my feelings. I understand myself better.
I understand my thinking. I understand my behavior.

Rhonda White

CHAPTER FOUR

Let's not give bad behavior a space to manifest
Change your behavior, change your life!

Rhonda White

BEHAVIOR JOURNALING

"Jot down seven behaviors that you would like to change"

1. _______________________________
2. _______________________________
3. _______________________________
4. _______________________________
5. _______________________________
6. _______________________________
7. _______________________________

Don't hide your power, don't hide your talent
Be the best version of you.
Be admired & respected!
To get there journal

Rhonda White

Dear Reader,

Welcome to Behavior Journaling. Put your feet up and stay awhile.

Think about simple and good things and then write about them in your journal. What is simple and good to you. What are the things that feel right in your life. Journal your behavior. Is it reflecting the best part of you. What do you need to change about your behavior?

Remember when you journal, write about your daily experiences, and this is going to have you contemplate all sorts of things. Journaling brings amazing results. Stay focused and write about one thing at a time, for the purposes of this book focus on your daily behavior.

The purpose of behavior journaling is to become mindful of all aspects of your behavior, Journal about small and simple tasks and what you do to remain calm throughout your day. Remember your behavior is probably very good when you solve problems, but how is your behavior when things don't go your way. This is where most behavior issues start.

Lastly for this journaling session, what situations tend to shut you down and cause your behavior to go off the charts? Be open and honest in your writing and behavior journaling will give you a calm mind. Journaling allows me, in some very special way to be all that I am and to embrace my spirituality. Behavior journaling allows me to write down my negative feelings and discard them and feel

better. When I do my journaling, I feel lighter, lifted. I feel
my spiritual identity.

CHAPTER FIVE

Face your behavior and face it now. Contemplating your behavior, thinking about it is applauding. Really. Giving attention to your behavior is essential. Now, it is tempting to say that thinking about your behavior is going to make it all better. Thinking about your behavior is going to wipe the slate clean but there is a lot more to it than this. Contemplating your behavior, really thinking about it, even meditating on it should be a practice in your life. However, while contemplating your behavior is not a cure to bad behavior, it is a move forward to good behavior. Only through the process of contemplation will you completely acknowledge that there is a desire to deepen thoughts on something that can be made better, much better. Your behavior is something that is eternally important it is your traveling life companion. Did you know that. Well, you know it now.

I'm not saying that your behavior must be a glowing figure in society. What I am saying is that your behavior must be thought about every single day. You must own your behavior. You must own the things you say and that you don't say, and you must own your actions and reactions. You can make your behavior respectful glimmers of society or you can make it the ghastly glimmers of society. It is up to you.

Behavior is a natural place for me to explore the person I have become. Behavior has always been a hot topic for me in life. As I mentioned earlier ever since a classmate threw a rock at the back of my head in class I have been fascinated by the concept of behavior. I couldn't believe someone could do that and as I have grown through the years, I am amazed at the behavior indecencies that I have experienced and that I see every day. It has granted me insight into myself and into the concept of behavior. Behavior is personal. Remember that dear reader. Behavior is transferred from you to someone else. Society is so connected with the hustle and bustle that society forgets about good behavior. The wider circle of accomplishment and success is your behavior, contemplating your behavior brings you closer to your inner self.

Perhaps you are someone who screams the answers to someone else's questions. Being contemplative allows me to present the vision of me yelling my answers to someone and asking myself if I like that part of me. Do I like the way I look in that vision. Am I happy the way I presented myself in that vision. Did I spread good behavior in that vision. If the answer is no for the most part then it is clear to assume that you must acquire the know-how to change that vision and change your behavior, period.

People, your behavior should always be in touch with

reality. Engage and respect people's ideas and opinions, it is a chance you may not agree with it but you don't own someone else's opinion or idea. Communication is the best thing because it creates honest behavior. Good conduct doesn't pretend to be anything that it isn't. It isn't mean. It is professional and respectful. It is not absent of integrity and above all it is not obnoxiously unprofessional. There is no reason to attack anyone for speaking their mind. A person who contemplates their behavior gives other people who have demonstrated bad behavior in the past a chance again. Forgive those with bad behavior and don't offer excuses for your bad behavior—face it and fix it.

Meditate and contemplate. Cultivate awareness and peace as you concentrate on the external you. Breathe naturally and clear your mind. The only thing to concentrate on is your behavior. Your mind is clear now and you are ably focused on your behavior. Do you like what you see. Do you like how you feel when you think of your behavior. Never join your emotions with your meditation. Stay focused on your behavior not on your emotions. Mindfulness meditation helps to control your emotions it can also help you to regulate your emotions. Concentrate only on your behavior. Are you happy with the situation that you are thinking about. If you are not, then journal, write your emotions down and how you felt when someone said something and how you reacted. Jot down emotions, situations and feelings and then jot down your behavior. Jot with freedom!

Always write in the first person and record your thoughts freely. Remember no one is going to judge your actions only you. Your inner experiences are reflections of occurrences which you have experienced. It is in this journal that you will capture the essence of your behavior. By writing close to the time when an event occurred, you can grab your behavior and see it, sense it, write it, read it back and change it, Record feelings, sensations, experiences and your attitude at the time. Remember focus. This must be as accurate as possible so that you may see first-hand your behavior. At the back of this book is a journal that has been created just for you so that you can contemplate on your behavior, meditate on it and write about it in your journal.

There is beauty in contemplation. But the contemplative dimension is a looking back dimension. It is not to become famous or special or to become important. It is a place for improvement and honesty and accurate recollection. It is a place of intensely thinking about something and coming to terms with it. In this case and for the purposes of this book, the contemplative dimension is a place for you to change your behavior. It is an experience of peace and love that is present at the heart of your faith. I must stress here the importance of relaxation. You must not be stressed out for that will block an accurate portrayal of your behavior. This calls for solitude. Personal revitalization is at the end of the contemplative dimension. It is a place that is waiting for you with insight and resolution and behavior that you can be proud of.

Take up an interest in your behavior dear reader and use the journal at the end of this book. You will see that journaling will help you change your behavior. And what happens when you change your behavior. You change your life. . . .

CHAPTER SIX

Face your behavior, dear reader. Face it. Fix it!

Facing your behavior is an attribute of good character that makes you worthy of deep respect and admiration. Facing your behavior is for the greater good of your soul. It takes enormous courage to come forth and admit that you have bad behavior, said things that you shouldn't have and to admit that you, alone, made yourself look bad. It takes bravery to look in the mirror.

Now your face can droop when you realize your behavior has been inexcusable. But it is when you do an about face and do something about your behavior that is when you are really turning your behavior around. If you turn your behavior around, you turn your life around. Even the most powerful people have suffered the consequences of their poor behavior. I salute, celebrate and applaud people who have had the courage to face their behavior and realize that behavior is not a game. I support those who come forward and condemn their bad behavior.

When you face your behavior, you begin to assess your situations and how your behavior may have been unacceptable and displeasing and offensive to others. Negative impacts negative. And remember something because I hear this all the time. Everyone wants to make money. Well people, listen up. Behavior has a lot to do with being a success. And, do you know that negative behavior is something that successful people avoid. There are so many conversations about what makes a person successful. Is it their wit their attire? The choices they make. All of this and more are what makes a person successful including their behavior. How you carry yourself in life is essential along with how you organize your day and your priorities. But this is the key; a big priority in your life is your behavior. Face it. Fix it. Live with it and love it. Be proud of your behavior, dear reader!

CHAPTER SEVEN

BEHAVIOR JOURNALING

"Jot down seven behaviors that you would like to change"

1. _______________________________

2. _______________________________

3. _______________________________

4. _______________________________

5. _______________________________

6. _______________________________

7. _______________________________

Rhonda White

Sometimes, I wonder why people don't act right. I thought long and hard about this and I journalized extensively. I wrote as directly as possible. I didn't allow anything to dull my memories. When I am with my journal, I begin to see things so differently. I leave my moments as they are and try to accurately remember them and after I read what I wrote, I feel something. I feel the absurdity of not understanding and then I feel the beauty of the moment because I understand it all now.

Never taint the reality of it all and just know that everything is discoverable. So, breathe and take it easy. Let the thoughts you have hit the paper. Release. Pledge to write down only what you see and feel. Struggling with your behavior has you struggling with your circumstances. You are safe from all ridicule and confrontation now. You have your journal with you. Write and release your thoughts and emotions. Let your negative feelings go.

Write everything about your behavior that you dread and then write what makes you happy about you. Do you like the way you handle someone else's behavior. Do you like the way you help someone figure things out. Do you like the outcome of things when you get fully involved in a situation?

Remember one more thing, if you are too tired to journal dear reader, let it go and get some rest. You can always journal tomorrow.

CHAPTER EIGHT

Everyone is on their own pursuit of happiness.

When you want to change a situation, you must allow yourself to really see the situation as it really is. This is the only way to truly try to understand someone's behavior. Taking someone else's perspective will help you understand their behavior. You, dear reader, have your own growth opportunities and they have theirs. How you get to yours will be different as to how someone else handles their opportunities.

We are a world of impressions. It is very difficult to walk the path someone else has traveled. It is almost impossible to feel what someone else is feeling and it is impossible to behave as someone else does. Although we are all judgmental one of the most useful things you can do, dear reader, is to be understanding when you look at honest hardworking people. You must realize that everyone goes through their own turmoil and their behavior reflects this. Stand in someone else's shoes and you may realize that you don't have it so bad!

The point here is that your behavior can enable you to make someone's life better. Isn't that what it is all about?

It takes courage to help someone else with their behavior because it takes courage to help yourself improve your behavior. Do not get stuck in a rut. If your behavior is not working for you, come up with a strategy to change it. If people you are hanging out with are making you upset and your behavior reflects this then change your friends. Change what you think will help you with positive energy. Make your goals manageable and your behavior will become manageable.

There will be times when you will clash with people on the job. This is normal. Clashing personalities exist in the business world and in your personal life. Behavior must be kept in check regardless of team conflicts or project constraints. This is all part of managing your behavior.

CHAPTER NINE

I remember one day I was wondering why it was so difficult to relate to people. It seemed as if everyone was in their own world and I wasn't even speaking the same language that they were. It was very troubling for me. I couldn't seem to communicate with anyone. I started thinking long and hard about it. What is the problem. Why can't anyone seem to understand what I am saying. It didn't seem as if I was breathing the same air as anyone else and then it hit me. I realized what the problem was. It was their behavior and probably mines, too.

It seemed as if someone else's behavior was impacting my world all the time and I was reacting to it. And, I began to realize that behavior teaches lessons. Let me explain, dear reader. Your behavior teaches someone else about your arrogance, your toleration and overall your human nature. You don't have to always cater to your own interests. Why do you have to be the first one in the elevator. Why can't you wait and hold the door for someone. What is wrong with allowing someone to merge over into another lane without you getting hostile. If someone has fewer packages than you do in the line at the market, why can't you let them go first. I am making a compelling argument that we all want the rest, the water and shade in life, but there is a feeling of self-reward when we can bring the water to someone who needs it. Dear reader, when you walk side by side with someone instead of running to get ahead of them, you feel better about yourself and your behavior.

When someone offers you a drink, take a few moments to sit down with them and converse. A little rest throughout your day is a good thing. You cannot always feel the heat and hardship in life.

Stop and look at the trees on the horizon. They are there, but the problem is you don't see them anymore because you are bogged down with so many things that your behavior will not allow you to see those trees. In other words, behavior can work against us. Good behavior is carrying the cooking pot for someone and sharing your food. When you are selfish, dear reader, the negativity steps in and it finishes you off. You must break the negative things that are happening in your life by being a better person and doing positive things. Share the food!

Behavior is triggered by so many things. Hurting feet, impatience, a heavy backpack pressing down on your shoulders, not having enough money in the bank, breaking up with a girlfriend or boyfriend and even down to lukewarm coffee. When you are an enthusiastic person in life, and you can help someone with their duties and struggles, your behavior changes and you begin to feel better about your problems because you are helping someone else improve their behavior.

Life is about establishing good behavior patterns. One good behavior brings along another good behavior. The story that needs to be told about good behavior is that it brings good things. It gives us resilience to handle things. In your life, dear reader, you will experience controversial issues but it is how you handle these issues that will make you who you are. This is where behavior comes into play. Your behavior can either make you or break you in life.

This is true. You can control your behavior and make sure that you act properly. Practice good behavior all the time and you may just avoid a lot of issues that you may otherwise have to contend with. If someone devalues you, it stays with you. However, it is your behavior that stays with them. How you handle the situation is what sets you apart from others. Understand that I am not saying have people-pleasing tendencies to be your best, but be proud of your behavior in all that you do!

Dear reader as you work to reform certain aspects of your behavior, I want to share with you behaviors I notice about myself to help you as you begin your journal journey.

My unhealthy behavior I struggle with saying no this behavior has always gotten in the way of my personal and professional agenda, another unhealthy behavior is my ability to stay on a healthy diet. So you understand dear reader no one is exempt from bad behavior. So, I say to you Change your behavior change your life you can do it!

Behavior is your personal boundary. It is your journey that teaches you, and it is the journey that will change your life. Take one step at a time and you will make it to your destination which will reveal your purpose.

Rhonda White

CHAPTER TEN

Behavior is a pulse that is measured against
Your actions it controls your every move.
Make sure you are
Moving in the right direction

Rhonda White

Our behavior is a reappearing visual in your life to everyone you encounter. Behavior has an attention attracting ability that accompanies you throughout your entire life. It motivates other people to listen to you, perhaps buy a product you are selling, to hire you, promote you and to be part of your life in some way, personally or professionally. Negative emotions, hatred, anger and jealousy will affect your behavior and it will show. Dear reader, you cannot just shake off your behavior and not acknowledge it. You must make the decision to change it. It will be the best decision of your life. Change your behavior, change your life. This has been the theme of this.

Your experiences, expectations and attitude must be

positive and inviting to push out the opposite emotions that make your behavior unbecoming. You must have positive and inviting behavior. The individual gains from motivating yourself must become your style and your preference for handling life. Individual characteristics make people different. Individual behavior makes people different, too.

Everyone has their own style of behavior. Most interesting to me is how people react to things. Reactional behavior is a very big deal and has become a source of fascination and explanation for centuries. Simply observing someone else react to something generates your own philosophies. As to how you would react to do the same thing. Feelings and views vary from person to person. The power of self-control varies from person to person as well.

We react to things according to our sensitivities to the thing that is going on in our lives, or the lives of people we love. Now, with that said, your behavior, dear reader goes along with your understanding Inclinations and sentiments.

This is a big part of journaling. I try to put myself in someone else's shoes all the time.

How would I feel if I were them facing what they are facing. Would I understand their behavior better. Would my behavior be better. Would my attitude and behavior be better. You see, attitude is as important as behavior and behavior is as important as attitude. Both attitude and behavior feed off one another. But, how can you begin to understand someone else's behavior when you can barely understand your own. Please do me the honor dear reader, and step into my last entry of behavior journaling.

CHAPTER ELEVEN

BEHAVIOR JOURNALING

"Jot down seven behaviors that you would like to change"

1. _______________________________________

2. _______________________________________

3. _______________________________________

4. _______________________________________

5. _______________________________________

6. _______________________________________

7. _______________________________________

There is something about journaling that makes a person feel good. Life isn't always perfect, and I am no stranger to this. And I am no stranger to journaling. Behavior journaling allows me to zero in on who I am, and who I am that people see.

Journaling has allowed me to appreciate life and perceive life differently. I behave differently without judgement. I don't want to judge anyone. Who am I to do that? I want to understand myself and see my behavior for what it truly is so that I make no mistake when I contemplate it. I want to change my behavior because I know that when I change my behavior, I change my life!

Journaling for me is a sanctuary. It is the place for goodness and truth. It is a place where I can be honest with myself without feeling that I am being challenged by society. Journaling feeds me and carries me along and opens my eyes to communication. I am happy when I journal. I feel as if I understand myself the best when I jot down things about myself and my behavior that I really didn't know before.

Journaling is a great escape. Begin by writing about everything that bothers you about your attitude and behavior. This is a great place to start. This will improve your self-awareness.

Remember that journaling will help you change your behavior because it creates self-awareness. You will be more cognizant of your feelings and how you react to situations. Journaling will lead you to positive attitude and behavior changes. Although there is a tendency to slide back to old behaviors, by journaling this won't happen. Keep writing and reading about your behavior you will begin to see yourself thru your writing.

I believe in journaling, so much that I have built in a journal for you at the end of this book. You will find a series of blank pages. I inspire you, dear reader, after you read this book take a pen and record your behavior every day. I have found it beneficial to jot your behavior down without using the computer. Writing about your behavior is called reality writing. Self-awareness, Affirmation is very important for you to understand your behavior. You must know what situations you are able to handle with five-star behavior and what situations you are not able to handle with five-star behavior.

Happy Journaling!

When I journal, it feels like a revelation. Behavior journaling has always taken me on a fascinating journey to the depths of my being and it is here I trek into the realms of my behavior. So now, dear reader, come with me on a journey elsewhere. We are about to do some journaling into the power of the other. We are about to see into someone else so that we may see inside someone else's behavior and try to understand them and better understand ourselves.

You are no longer you from this point on. You are now someone else. For the purpose of this exercise. I will show you the process.

I am BB, an artistic woman from a middle-class neighborhood in a snow-covered section of the US. I am in a toxic relationship with my boyfriend and I don't care for my current administrative position in the city. I love art and would much rather stay at home and paint beautiful lobby murals for the lobbies of some of the finest hotels.

It is a cold blustery morning and I am already running late. My boyfriend and I are not speaking. My attitude is already formulated this morning by a few spats. I don't feel motivated or happy. I arrive to work and I am running around geting ready for my day. A co-worker approaches me with a smile, and I don't say good morning, but I don't have time to think about it. My co-worker is a bit offended, I can tell. Who cares, I think to myself as I race on with my aimless go nowhere obligations. I could be home in a warm apartment, painting. Do you see, dear reader, when you look in someone's life you can understand their behavior. The problem is, you really don't have the opportunity to see into someone's life like you just did.

This is BB. Now, dear reader, you are aware that BB has a lot going on in her life. She has all the ingredients for her to display bad behavior. BB really may be leading a meaningful life, but she doesn't see it and it is showing in her behavior. BB small insignificant behavior to a co-worker was hurtful to the co-worker. BB did not say good morning, if she had, it would have been returned with a smile. You would be surprised how good behavior can change someone else's day. A nurse could have changed a patient's day if she would have just given that patient a smile. A co-worker can help a team efforts by saying some positive words of encouragement. I think you get the picture, dear reader. Good behavior goes a very long way.

This part of behavior journaling has you focusing on the other person for a reason. The world does not revolve around you, dear reader, but it does interact with your behavior. You can reduce your negative emotions and improve your behavior by taking a few moments and journaling the way I just did. It allows you to be able to see someone and how they act a bit differently. Be understanding and patient and kind. Formulate a narrative guide, like I just did. It will allow you to see into someone else's life and understand their behavior better and your own.

My Behavior is my journey thank you
for being a part of it.
It is through you I can see me!

Rhonda White

· · · · · · · · · · · · ·

Stress is all over the place
It is not easy to stay calm
It is hard to stay focused
But remember to see and smell the roses
Change your behavior to change your life

Rhonda White

CHAPTER TWELVE

Where would I be without God. I need him in every
Single moment of my life, you need him in
Every single moment of your life, the world needs him.

Rhonda White

God is part of everything I do. You see, everyone experiences difficulties of one type or another. Some have financial difficulties and others are handling chronic stress of perhaps a divorce, a crumbling marriage, a death or educational issues. Stressors no matter what, they may hit all of us. Include me in this equation as well. I've had my share of stressors.

God has played a big part in my life, providing me a sense of hope despite any situations I contend with in life. God has guided my steps during times of uncertainty which has helped me through unfamiliar places.

God has been my starting point and has instilled in me the importance of faith and the importance of good behavior.

God gives me my appetite for life. God provides me with a deeper understanding of virtually everything. God pushes me to better myself in this world every single day. God allows me to see the importance of a sense of humor and that I should be passionate about making someone smile. I think my relationship with God reveals itself in me practicing good behavior. And when I journal, I project these intentions onto my pages. It is this sense of engagement with God that makes me feel love, kindness and joy.

God helps me when the clouds seem to circle around me and I feel overwhelmed and confused. When I feel judged and let down, God fills me with eager enthusiasm and lets me know that I have the ability, alone, to accomplish what I need to accomplish. But most of all we have a sympathetic and compassionate God who understands and helps me find the words that I need to feel the best about who I am as a person.

I tend to keep worry out by keeping faith in. Faith is my introductory note to all things and is in my conclusions about all things. Faith fills me with good cheer and seem to always dry my tears. Faith enlightens me with commonsense thinking and optimism. It allows me to be reasonable and caring and give respect to all including myself. Respect, faith and love is the ticket to good living and to "Golden Behavior. Now what do I mean by golden behavior. Read on dear reader!

Golden behavior knowing that God is with me when I have been reasonable and rational in all that I have done and in all that I will continue to do. I am doing my best to prevent hurt and harm to others. I am keeping and maintaining the thoughts and feelings of those I know and don't know closely. I am kind to the elderly and to the unfortunate. I am a blessing to where and when I can be in someone else's life. I embrace the peaceful flow of good behavior and good care to this planet. I am clear in my spirit because faith fills each moment of my day.

My behavior offers kindness to those who are all nerves and who are going through difficult times. My conduct allows me to be centered and avoid the extremes of my emotions. I dont feel jealousy or envy because they cloud my behavior. I cherish joy and pray that it is inside of my heart and releases out into my bloodstream and carries me on a behavior path that enlightens those around me. Worry is in my brain, but faith is in my heart and God is in my life and so my behavior is golden!

God gives me strength and my strength gives me commitment and consistency. And my faith scatters my energy so wherever I go, whatever I do, whatever highway I drive my horizons are clear in all directions and do you know why. It's my faith. It is the who, what, and when and why in my life. Faith allows me to let down my stress and be pleasant to work and to live with and be a good friend. And do you know something, dear reader, Faith allows me to be a good friend to me, love and honor myself in every way it also allows me to give myself a pat on the back. My behavior is golden to those around me

In the rushing around of life, the exam taking, the business making and the subway taking, faith rushes around with me. The great highway may be society's symbol of power and progress, but I keep myself grounded in the crowd and the pushing and shoving because it is my faith that pushes me on, and it is God that I go to at the end of my day for my sensible conclusions.

If I have hugged and held and consoled, If I have extended kindness to all living things and if I have embraced my faith and God proudly, respectfully and lovingly then my behavior is golden and my life is headed in the right direction.

We seem to measure everything by the dollar standard, so to speak, and count our pennies. Unfortunately success is not measured by what we made and not so much how we earned it. The mountain is there. Climb the mountain top every day in all that you do. Breathe free. Love God. Be kind. And strive not just for good behavior but for golden behavior and cherish your faith in all that you do.

I thought about putting it off
Changing my behavior
Would take too much time
It would require too much thought
I wanted to procrastinate.
But I saw how easy it was
To change my behavior
And do you know something?
It changed my life!

Rhonda White

Dear Reader,

I think it is evident that bad behavior does not rock. It is irritating, annoying, a real turn-off and to be rather blunt about it, it pisses people off. If you want to make enemies, bad behavior does the trick. Now, while it is not cool to judge someone right off the bat, offensive behavior leaves a bad impression and you can spot it right away. Now sure, a person is entitled to a bad day, but bad behavior leaves an impression that can stick with you for the rest of your life. Seriously, you must be prepared for someone bringing up an offensive thing you did or said years later and why is this. The answer is clear; it is because of your behavior.

Unfortunately, bad behavior sticks to someone's memory and when an executive must make a choice whether to keep you on your job or keep the other person, he or she might just keep the other person because of the way you may have acted or something offensive you said. So, if you want to be a superstar at the office you may want to watch your behavior. There's a simple lesson here and that is you have no idea how much your behavior influences another person's judgement. It never made sense to me that someone would achieve any kind of success in show business, in the corporate realm or in their personal life by being a jerk.

Remember something, dear reader, disrespect brings on disrespect. Disrespect invites disrespect. You can single-handedly destroy your career ladies and gentlemen by being uncouth. You either get approving nods in life or disapproving looks. It is up to you. I cannot make it clearer. Bad behavior generally ensures a short shelf life to any career. The question is really, what kind of person do you want to be. What kind of person do you want to be climbing that corporate ladder. How do you want to be remembered. It is in your control. Yes. Dear reader, your behavior is in your control.

I hope it has been apparent as a result of reading this book that you have seen, dear reader, how important your behavior is to your advancement in life. This book has been written so that you may improve your position in life. Behavior realizations have been plentiful in these pages. Your behavior has a strong impact on your life. Behavior management problems will slow you down, in the business world and not only make you someone that people want to avoid in their life.

Offensive behavior is embarrassing to everyone. When you are offensive you give off bad vibes. As a matter of fact, a celebrity's bad behavior is linked to a bad movie. And if you don't think so think about how celebs have been pushed off the screen by their offensive behavior. Don't think bad behavior doesn't catch up with you. It will one way or another and if by chance, if it is not in this life it will come back at you when you least expect it, somewhere out there!

Why is it that amazing talent is sometimes accompanied by bad behavior. The amazing talent would even be more amazing if it did not accompany it. The angry berating person that goes around squabbling and demanding this and that executes behavior that is very difficult to ignore. Sure, they may make lots of money and appear successful, but they are not highly regarded. It is hard to ignore the uncompromising difficult individual whose obnoxious demeanor is rooted in conduct that creates a toxic workplace and abusive one that you must work in daily. And that toxicity that you absorb every day, you take home with you and you release it in your personal life. Poor conduct goes on and on and leaves a trail of bread crumbs.

The frustrating work environment is toxic and spreads and contaminates every aspect of your life. You react to the frustration. The assumption has always been that bad behavior is just part of doing business and that you must protect your ego and just suck it up. You can be confident that the environment of people angrily yelling at one another is not a positive environment to be in and certainly not a positive environment for you to pass on to friends and loved ones. Look at your life. Look at someone else's behavior and ask yourself, do you want to look like that. Bad behavior people are a spectacle and to be sure, bad behavior is not people you want to hang around. They have been affected by the epidemic of bad behavior. Don't hang out with them. They are not pleasant people. Bad behavior has seen to that!

Economic injustice, political corruption and pretty much the raw stuff of American culture is revealed by the way someone acted in a situation that he or she just couldn't live down. In other words, no matter who you are, bad behavior opens a huge can of worms. The fractures of your life, the broken-up moments you experience crack open with rougher points and sharper edges by just what you say and do. Professional behavior in your personal life is a must. Personal behavior in your professional life is a must.

Images, language, ideas, implications, opinions are dubbed to your character like gum on the bottom of your shoe. But you can operate under rules of your own. No one is stopping you, but you. Decency is in your future and you don't need a crystal ball to see it. You just need to look in the mirror and say, I want to change. I don't want to be like this anymore. I want to have a better life. I want to make life better for others.

Break someone's spirit. Anyone can destroy someone's vision with their bad behavior. Do you want that on you. Is that your legacy. Dear reader, is that what you want to leave behind for your children, your friends and family members. Do you want to be known for your bad behavior and remembered by it. When it comes time to leaving this world your legacy is what you will leave behind. Bad behavior should not be your legacy.

I must say this strongly, if you want to corner the market on crazy, bad behavior will do it for you. You cannot go off because of a set of uncivilized notions you somehow seem to walk around with and exhibit. You've got to get rid of those notions that have no moral gravity to them. No one is going to see your talent if all they can see is your bad behavior. Remember the best way for people formulate a good opinion about you is if they see you in a good light. Behavior is the switch for you to turn on. Bad behavior is a turn off, big time. You can live well, dear reader, if you change your behavior in every ordeal; even the ones that make you shake your head in dismay.

Behavior is the dynamic of your spirit. It is how you move through life. It is what people see and it is what they remember. Whether you fly or fall, depends on your behavior. Behavior can be many things. Behavior is how you choose to respond to situations that you are confronted with in all that you do. Behavior dictates attitude. Behavior is the external, it is what we show.

Behavior shows in our performance whether it is mentally, physically or emotionally and bad behavior has become a movement and society's biggest blemish that cannot be covered up. Get your behavior together, people. Behavior is your gift start your day with a smile. Greet it with a smile and embrace it with good behavior.

Be someone people want to be around. Be a person who values others. Be the person who supports someone in their good and bad times. Be a friend and show your positive behavior in relating to others. Show kindness to all living things.

And dear reader, just know that you are on the journey to change your behavior change your life.

I am Rhonda White. Thank you for reading.

EPILOGUE

Dear Reader,

Good behavior brings good choices. Start your journal journey no matter where you are in your life, good or bad place it doesn't matter. Watch things begin to unfold. Create a bucket list of good behaviors you would like to possess. Live them own them and magnify and glorify them in majestic way. Use this behavioral journey as your personal connection to you. Take time to spend with yourself. Love the gift of life that God has given us, and share it with someone lets pass the torch of good behavior.

The point is, regardless of the outcome of our decisions, we must be able to wear our decisions well. We must do what! Change our behavior change our life.

Rhonda White

BEHAVIOR JOURNALING

"Change your behavior, change your life"

\
\
\
\

BEHAVIOR JOURNALING

"Change your behavior, change your life"

\
\
\
\

BEHAVIOR JOURNALING

"Change your behavior, change your life"

BEHAVIOR JOURNALING

"Change your behavior, change your life"

BEHAVIOR JOURNALING

"Change your behavior, change your life"

BEHAVIOR JOURNALING

"Change your behavior, change your life"

BEHAVIOR JOURNALING

"Change your behavior, change your life"

BEHAVIOR JOURNALING

"Change your behavior, change your life"

BEHAVIOR JOURNALING

"Change your behavior, change your life"

____

____

____

____

BEHAVIOR JOURNALING

"Change your behavior, change your life"

____

____

____

____

____

PERSONAL AFFIRMATION

"As a part of your journal create a personal affirmation"